THE FJH
CONTEMPORARY
KEYBOARD
EDITIONS

Piano Sonata No.4

Op.128

Edited by Diane Andersen

Series editor: Helen Marlais

Dianne Goolkasian Rahbee

Production: Frank J. Hackinson
Production Coordinator: Philip Groeber
Cover: Terpstra Design, San Francisco
Cover Painting: Klamm Improvisation, 1914, W. Kandinsky
Engraving: Tempo Music Press, Inc.
Printer: Tempo Music Press, Inc.

ISBN 1-56939-494-6

Copyright © MMVI by
THE FJH MUSIC COMPANY INC.
2525 Davie Road, Suite 360
Fort Lauderdale, FL 33317-7424
International Copyright Secured.
All Rights Reserved. Printed in U.S.A.

THE
F·J·H
MUSIC
COMPANY
INC.

Frank J. Hackinson

Notes from the Composer

The character of the *Sonata No. 4* is extremely positive in nature, describing the personality of the artist for whom it was written, Diane Andersen. The "Diane" motive (D-D♭) descending half step, is found throughout the Sonata along with the initials of both the composer and Ms. Andersen, D. A. and D. G. that have a very dominant musical relationship.

The first movement, marked *maestoso,* must be played with feelings of great happiness. The first theme is a rapturous introduction to the contemplative melodic second theme of the "Diane" motive. The development section plays with material from the exposition and is followed by the recapitulation and coda.

The second movement, marked, *molto energico e presto,* is to be played with joy and excitement. The third movement, *molto espressivo e rubato,* is a highly emotional movement that can be played with a lot of rubato. It has also been arranged for various instrumental combinations at the request of performers.

The last movement, the *Toccata,* is to be performed with boundless energy. This movement is a wild display of energetic release and may be performed as a separate piece.

I hope you will enjoy playing this work as much as I enjoyed composing it!

Sincerely,
Dianne Goolkasian Rahbee

About the Composer

Dianne Goolkasian Rahbee, born in Somerville, Massachusetts, February 9, 1938, is a first generation Armenian-American whose father was a survivor of the genocide, and much of her music reflects a deep-rooted ethnic background. The strong influences of her first spoken language, Armenian, and of the folk music in the home where she grew up, are important elements in her musical language. Her early love for music was sparked by her mother, a talented violinist.

Dianne began her musical training as a pianist in Boston with Antoine Louis Moeldner, who studied with two of Leschetitzky's most illustrious pupils, Helen Hopekirk and Paderewski. The Moeldner-Hopekirk connection would have particular impact: Moeldner had been a teaching assistant to Ossip Gabrilovich, while Helen Hopekirk was herself a highly respected composer and pianist, and served as an early role model for Goolkasian Rahbee. The influence of this distinguished lineage was a powerful inspiration. She continued her studies at Juilliard as a piano major and at Mozarteum in Salzburg, Austria studying chamber music with Enrico Mainardi. In later years, Dianne studied piano privately with David Saperton in New York and Lily Dumont, Russell Sherman, and Veronica Jochum in Boston. As a self-taught composer, she began writing pieces for her piano students and received encouragement to continue this work from Constance Keene and David Saperton, among others.

At age 40, Goolkasian Rahbee began concentrating on composing, and has since produced a large body of works for piano solo, orchestra, instrumental ensembles, percussion, and voice. Her music is performed internationally, and many large festivals have featured her works in the U.S. and abroad.

About the Editor

Diane Andersen, referred to as the "Grand Lady of the Belgian Piano" by the international press and considered to be a remarkably complete musician, is making a brilliant career both as a concert pianist and a pedagogue. While Andersen has championed Belgian music the world over, her repertoire also includes works by early composers such as Cherubini and Kozeluch, performed on the pianoforte, to romantic and contemporary composers, several of whom have written especially for her. A recipient of many international awards: "FUGA" Trophy (Union of Belgian Composers), honoured with the "Harriet Cohen International Bach-Medal" (London) and "Grand Prix du Disque de l'Académie Charles Cros" (Paris), Diane Andersen has performed with such renowned conductors as Maderna, Boulez, and Sawallisch, and collaborated with composers Kodály and Tansman. Her discography is very impressive with interesting LPs and numerous CDs in first world performances (works by Tansman, Kodály, Milhaud, Bartók, Kozeluch, Cherubini, etc.) receiving wide acclaim by the press. Her last CD with works by Belgian composer Adolphe Biarent received the "Cannes Classical Award" at the Cannes MIDEM Festival, January 2003.

Andersen is a professor at the renowned "Conservatoire Royal de Musique" in Brussels, and serves on the jury of important international competitions. Along with being president of the European Piano Teacher's Association, she is president for the piano competition for young pianists and is artistic director of the master course, "The International Piano Week" in Belgium.

Visit her web-site:
http://diane-andersen.org

Performer's Notes

Much has already been said and written about Dianne Goolkasian Rahbee's music, but to me its most important quality is the conciseness of ideas; the Fourth Piano Sonata being a very good example of this. Goolkasian Rahbee does not need lots of pages to express her deepest feelings. Each part of the sonata is an emotional world in itself, depicting in a few seconds, a lifetime's experience of love, passion, tenderness, anger, and even rebellion! Dianne Goolkasian Rahbee's great art exists because of the choice of her compositional material. All the ingredients are simple, making the music easy to play yet very effective. Each performer has the freedom to display his or her technical and emotional brilliance; no struggle with the keyboard, nothing complicated, only the joy of playing. This sonata holds treasures – visible and hidden. It makes each performance a new discovery and pleasure. Enjoy it!

Brussels, July 10, 2004

Diane Andersen

Series Editor

Helen Marlais has given collaborative recitals throughout the U.S. and in Canada, Italy, France, Germany, Turkey, Hungary, Lithuania, Russia, and China. She is recorded on Gasparo and Centaur record labels, and has performed and given workshops at local, state and national music teachers' conventions, including the National Conference on Keyboard Pedagogy and the National Music Teacher's convention. She is Director of Keyboard Publications for the FJH Music Company and her articles can be read in major keyboard journals.

Dr. Marlais is an associate professor of piano at Grand Valley State University in Grand Rapids, MI. She has also held full-time faculty piano positions at the Crane School of Music, S.U.N.Y. at Potsdam, Iowa State University, and Gustavus Adolphus College.

for Diane Andersen

Piano Sonata

I

Dianne Goolkasian Rahbee
No. 4, Op. 128

Maestoso (♩ = ca. 72)
with feelings of great happiness

bring out top notes of R.H. chords

Meno mosso e rubato
molto espressivo

Più mosso e poco agitato

II

16

III

20

J1014

IV

* play as if gradually **aw**akening from a dream

* play as if gradually awakening from a dream